What Charlotte Found at Seneca Falls

A Story of the First Woman's Rights Convention

by
Elizabeth Weiss Vollstadt

Illustrated by Vivian Saad

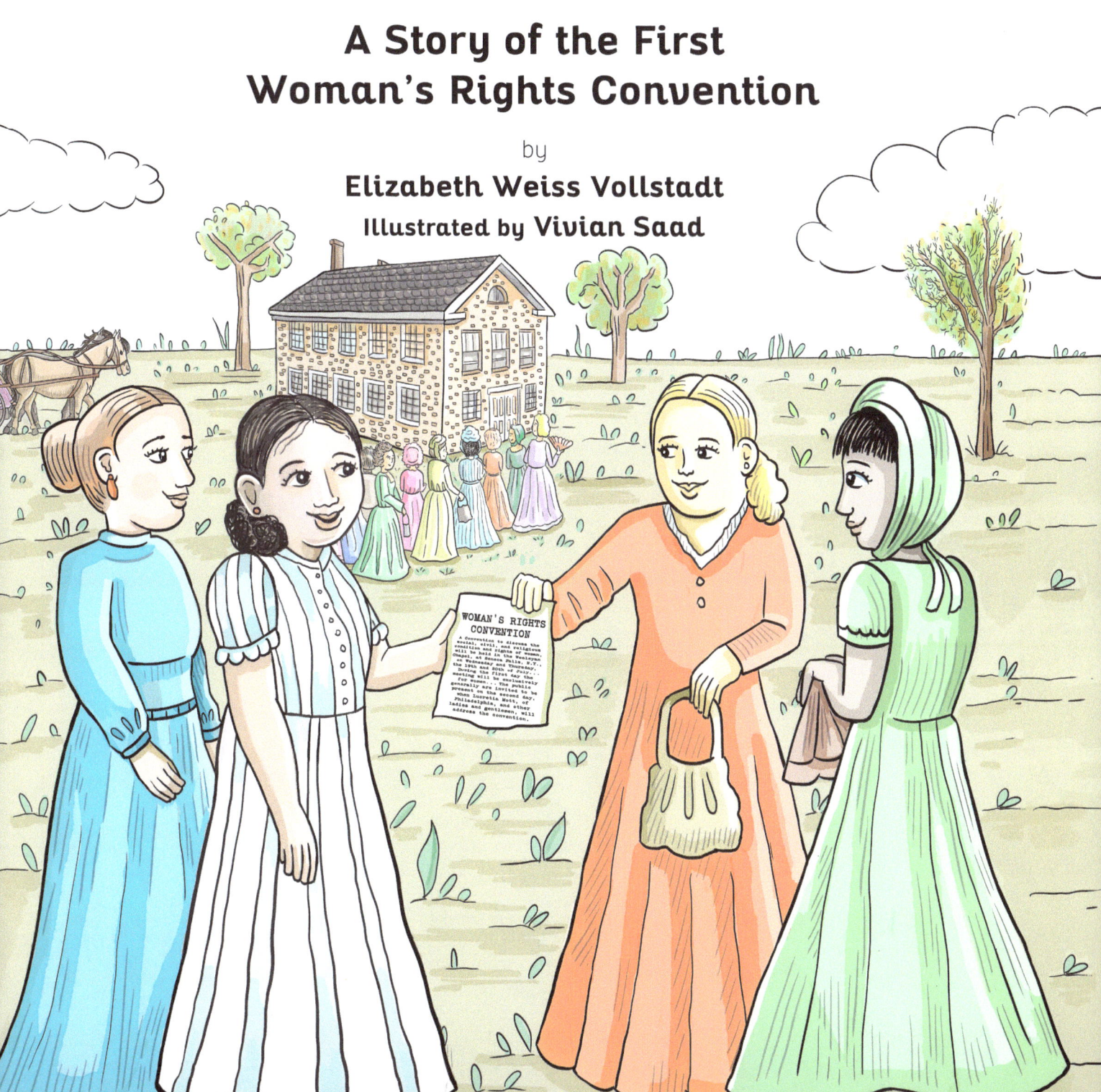

Also by the Author:

Young Patriots
Inspiring Stories of the American Revolution

Pairs on Ice

Pairs at Nationals

Copyright © 2025 by Elizabeth W. Vollstadt. All rights reserved
ISBN: 979-8-9989897-2-8

All rights reserved. Except for use in a review, the reproduction or use of this work in whole or in part, in any form by any electronic, mechanical, or other means, now known or hereafter invented, including xerography, photocopying, and recording, or in any information storage or retrieval system, is forbidden without the written permission of the author.

www.elizabethvollstadt.com
www.amazon.com/author/elizabethvollstadt
lizwrites28@gmail.com

To my granddaughter, Amelia, and all of today's strong young women who will continue the march toward full equality begun so many years ago at Seneca Falls.

Charlotte Woodward hated to sew. It didn't matter. Every day her needle went in and out of soft leather pieces, turning them into gloves for fine ladies to wear. How she longed to do something else! Even hanging laundry would be less dreary. Why couldn't she do a task she wanted — like work in a print shop. She could make words instead of gloves.

But that was impossible.

7

Girls didn't apprentice in trades.
They didn't work in shops.
They didn't go to college.

Most girls accepted this as God's will, the way things were meant to be.
But not Charlotte.

I do not believe, she thought, *that there was any community anywhere in which the souls of some women were not beating their wings in rebellion.*

She knew *her* wings were beating. But they couldn't lift her off the ground.

Until . . .

One day, July 11, 1848, she picked up the *Seneca County Courier*. Her eyes opened wide when she read,

> WOMAN'S RIGHTS CONVENTION.
>
> A Convention to discuss the social, civil, and religious condition and rights of woman, will be held in the Wesleyan Chapel, at Seneca Falls, N.Y., on Wednesday and Thursday, the 19th and 20th of July... During the first day the meeting will be exclusively for women... The public generally are invited to be present on the second day, when Lucretia Mott, of Philadelphia, and other ladies and gentlemen, will address the convention.

Charlotte knew she had to go.

She dashed outside to spread the news. Not everyone shared her excitement. Some women scowled. They said they were too busy to worry about rights. Others laughed. But Charlotte found a few friends who agreed to go to Seneca Falls with her.

One day, July 11, 1848, she picked up the *Seneca County Courier*. Her eyes opened wide when she read,

> WOMAN'S RIGHTS CONVENTION.
>
> A Convention to discuss the social, civil, and religious condition and rights of woman, will be held in the Wesleyan Chapel, at Seneca Falls, N.Y., on Wednesday and Thursday, the 19th and 20th of July... During the first day the meeting will be exclusively for women... The public generally are invited to be present on the second day, when Lucretia Mott, of Philadelphia, and other ladies and gentlemen, will address the convention.

Charlotte knew she had to go.

She dashed outside to spread the news. Not everyone shared her excitement. Some women scowled. They said they were too busy to worry about rights. Others laughed. But Charlotte found a few friends who agreed to go to Seneca Falls with her.

On July 19th, the girls set out early. They drove through woods and plodded past fields of golden wheat.
At first, they were alone. Would they be alone at the Convention, too?

But soon another wagon joined them. Then more wagons came. They formed a small procession.

Finally they arrived in Seneca Falls. A large crowd mingled outside the chapel.

Why were the doors shut? Did the minister change his mind about allowing a woman's rights convention?
Maybe so, but the women would not be stopped. Charlotte saw a young man boosted up to a window. He pried open a shutter, climbed in, and opened the door. The Convention could begin.

Elizabeth Cady Stanton, one of the day's organizers, spoke first. She read from a paper. Her hands trembled, but her voice rang out clear and strong.

"When in the course of human events it becomes necessary..." The familiar words of the Declaration of Independence filled the chapel. "We hold these truths to be self-evident, that all men **and women** are created equal... that they are endowed by their Creator with certain unalienable Rights."

Charlotte's whole being sang at hearing the words "and women." Then, just as the Declaration of Independence listed grievances against England's King George, this new declaration listed women's grievances against men.

Some wrongs Charlotte already knew, like being denied an education or a choice of professions. Others hadn't touched her yet.

Men forbade women to speak in public.

They passed laws that women were no longer considered separate persons when they married. Everything a married woman had—her clothing, her property, her wages, her children—belonged to her husband.

And . . . they denied women the right to vote, which meant they couldn't change the laws that harmed them. Charlotte sighed. All this was true, but what could this small group of women do?

In the afternoon, she found out. Mrs. Stanton presented proposals, called resolutions, to correct each of these wrongs. Universities should open their doors to women, declared one. Another said that marriage should not take away a woman's right to be an independent person. And women must be allowed to vote.

The next day, the resolutions were approved with no opposition.
Except one.

It was the demand for the right to vote.
One man said women voting would destroy families.
A woman believed they could change laws without voting. Even Mrs. Mott had said, "Why Lizzie, thee will make us ridiculous."
But Mrs. Stanton persisted. At first she stood alone. All alone.

Then a tall black man stood up. He was Frederick Douglass, a former slave, now a writer and speaker.

"With respect to political rights," he said, "we hold that woman should be justly entitled to all we claim for man."

Although some people voted no, the resolution passed. Now it was time to sign a statement of agreement—the Declaration of Sentiments. Would people sign their names for all to see?

Charlotte signed.

Sixty-eight women and thirty-two men signed.

But not everyone.

Charlotte thought they were afraid. The resolutions called on them to follow a new path. Maybe they preferred to stay on the familiar one.

News of the Convention spread. A St. Louis newspaper wrote, "The flag of independence has been hoisted for the second time on this side of the Atlantic."

But another newspaper called it "a petticoat rebellion, arranged by love-starved spinsters."

Many signers of the Declaration took back their signatures. But not Charlotte.

Charlotte now knew she was not alone. Hope rose in her like the sun over the hills. Soon, she found the courage to change her life. Charlotte stopped sewing gloves. She learned to be a typesetter. At first, no one would hire her. They wanted a man.

But Charlotte did not give up.
She found a printer to hire her. The printer was a woman, Amelia Bloomer. Amelia published a feminist newspaper, *The Lily*, in Seneca Falls. Now Charlotte could help bring women's rights to the world.

Charlotte no doubt gave up printing when she married and became Mrs. Newlin Pierce. But she remained active in the growing woman's rights movement.

The battle was long. The Nineteenth Amendment granting women the right to vote wasn't ratified until many years later in 1920. Charlotte was the only person still living who had signed the Declaration of Sentiments at Seneca Falls. She was now ninety-one years old.

How wonderful it would be to say that Charlotte proudly cast her vote that year. But she did not. She became ill and could not go to the polls. The following year, her eyesight failed. "I'm too old," she said. "I'm afraid I'll never vote."

As far as we know, she never did. But over the past one hundred years, millions of women have voted for her.

The end

More About Charlotte

Charlotte Woodward Pierce, to use her married name, was not a leader in the suffrage movement. She did not organize the Seneca Falls Woman's Rights Convention. That honor belongs to Elizabeth Cady Stanton, Lucretia Mott and their friends Martha Coffin Wright, Mary Ann M'Clintock, and Jane Hunt. They were all already active in the abolitionist movement to end slavery.

Charlotte Woodward was just a teenaged girl who hated to sew gloves, but still spent hours sewing pieces together. Why? Because there were so few ways for her to earn money. Even working in a factory was not accepted in her community. Instead, women did piece work at home. Companies like the glove makers in Gloversville, New York, sent leather pieces already cut for women to sew together. They earned a small sum for each glove made, money that belonged to their father if they were under 21 or husband if they were married.

No wonder Charlotte's "wings were beating in rebellion." How happy she must have been to read about a Woman's Rights Convention not too far from home. She didn't know what to expect. She probably didn't think it would change her life. But it did. Not only did she find the courage to stop sewing gloves, but she supported women's rights her entire life. She joined the American Woman Suffrage Association and the American Association for the Advancement of Women.

But surely, Charlotte was not the only one whose life changed at Seneca Falls. It is likely that the Convention was a turning point for many women—forever unknown—who found hope and joined the movement.

Soon more and more women gained a new respect for themselves and came to believe that they, too, were "endowed by their Creator with certain unalienable Rights." They held meetings, went to conferences, marched in the streets, picketed the White House. The right to vote was not "given" to women. They fought for it, year after year, refusing to give up, until the Nineteenth Amendment passed on August 18, 1920.

All girls and women today stand on the shoulders of the early feminists when they vote, own their own businesses, work for good wages, enter a profession, serve in the United States Senate, and see themselves as Vice-President or even President. They have climbed higher than Charlotte and the other women of Seneca Falls could ever imagine. And if young girls today keep up the fight for equality, they will reach even greater heights.

Acknowledgements

Writing may be a solitary profession, but producing a book takes a village. So here are my thank yous to the village that helped me along the way.

First, I'd like to thank the people at the Women's Rights Historical National Park in Seneca Falls, New York. Every July they sponsor a celebration of the 1848 Woman's Rights Convention. When I first started thinking about this book, I was fortunate to attend the 2019 Convention Days. There I listened to talks about women's history and had a chance to meet Coline Jenkins, Elizabeth Cady Stanton's great-great granddaughter, who is following her family's tradition as she supports women's rights today, and historian Judith Wellman, Principal Investigator, Historical New York Research Associates, and Professor Emerita, State University of New York at Oswego. Judith was kind enough to read the manuscript for historical accuracy and offer comments and suggestions. Any errors are mine alone.

Many thanks also to Jennifer Hasse, Head of Access Services and Student Experience at Saint Joesph's University Libraries, Philadelphia, PA. Jen used her skills to find Rheta Childe Door's interview with 91-year-old Charlotte Woodward that appeared in the magazine Colliers: The National Weekly, on October 30, 1920. The article, called "The Eternal Question," gave me unique insights into Charlotte's thoughts as she remembered the convention so many years ago.

And I can't forget my talented illustrator, Vivian Saad, whose lovely illustrations brought Charlotte to life. Then there is fellow writer and dear friend, Barbara Whittington, who not only read my drafts but is always there to offer support and encouragement. Children's poetry writer Jill Clark is another friend who read and critiqued several drafts.

Lastly, I am so grateful to have a husband who is always willing to accompany me on research trips and traipse around historical sites. Thank you, Peter, for being you.

Elizabeth Vollstadt

History was never Elizabeth Vollstadt's favorite subject until she discovered women's history and could see herself in their lives. Her earliest published stories for children featured strong brave girls in history—some real, some fictional—who weren't afraid to stand up for themselves and others. Elizabeth is delighted to share this story of the 1848 Seneca Falls Woman's Rights Convention with today's girls. She lives in New Jersey, not far from Philadelphia, where she is now researching true stories about women during the American Revolution. You can reach her at www.elizabethvollstadt.com

Vivian Saad

Vivian Saad illustrates children's and young adult books. She has a Bachelor's Degree in Graphic Design from the University Belas Artes of São Paulo, and currently lives in Brazil. She has illustrated more than seventy books and has participated in exhibitions and catalogs in countries such as Argentina, Canada, Australia, and the United States. Vivian's illustrations capture the emotions and experiences that bond us as humans. To contact Vivian and view more of her work, visit: http://www.viviansaadilustras.com